Copyright © 2022 Natasha Boyd

All rights reserved. No portion of this book may be reproduced in any form without permission from the publisher, except as permitted by U.S. copyright law. For permissions contact: pragmaticslady@yahoo.com or The Pragmatics Lady 5050 Laguna Blvd. Suite 112-718 Elk Grove, CA 95758

Written and edited by Natasha Boyd

Published by Get It Girl Publishing

Printed in the United States of America

Paperback
ISBN: 978-1-7345270-3-2

PRAGMATICS

It's not what you say, it's how you say it

By:
Natasha Boyd

About Pragmatics

Pragmatics deals with the actual behavior that is exhibited during communication, such as eye contact, eye rolling, and hand gestures. 93% of communication is nonverbal, this also includes attire and punctuality.

- **<u>WHAT WE SAY WITHOUT SAYING A WORD</u>**
  When inappropriate pragmatics behaviors accompany words, mixed messages can occur. Pragmatics (without words, often speak loudly to your listener)

- **<u>BEING AWARE OF YOUR PRAGMATICS (MODELING INAPPROPRIATELY)</u>**
  People watch the behavior of others. If they observe inappropriate behaviors, they will not have clear models to imitate. By modeling appropriate pragmatics, clear concise message without mixed communication is given.

- **<u>ALLOWING PEOPLE TO BECOME AWARE OF THEIR OWN PRAGMATIC BEHAVIORS</u>**
  When specific pragmatic behaviors (i.e eye rolling, loud tone) are pointed out and discussed, people are then able to understand the message they send to their listener.

- **<u>TEACHING PEOPLE TO BECOME ACCURATE JUDGES OF NON-VERBAL MESSAGES</u>**
  When people begin to be aware of the pragmatics of others, it allows them to get their needs and desires met through the communication process.

Accurate reading of non-verbal cues will result in fewer confrontations with students, teachers, peers, parents, and employers.

Don't take our word for it. Try the techniques for yourself.

Ms. Pragmatics

Hello!

Allow me to introduce myself, my name is The Pragmatics Lady or TPL for short and you will see me throughout the workbook. I am here to introduce you to the benefits of pragmatics. You will find activities and information that will help you become a stronger communicator. Oftentimes our nonverbal communication is ignored, and we just focus on words. However, 93% of information is nonverbal so it's time to pay attention to your pragmatics. By the end of this workbook, you will become "Pragmatized." That means you will become familiar with what you say nonverbally to others and what others are saying nonverbally to you. I hope this workbook helps you to examine your communication patterns and feel confident in whatever speaking communication environment you are in. I do not want you to become "The Pragmatics Lady", I just want you to be the best communicator you can be.

PRAGMATICS CULPRITS

- Facial Expressions
- Facial Grimaces
- Eye rolling
- Head nodding
- Body posturing (slumping, slouching, etc.)
- Turning your head and/or body away from the speaker
- Sucking in air
- Blowing out air loudly
- Pitch and Tone of voice
- Sing–song voice
- Inflections and volume of the voice
- Invasion of personal body space
- Hand and arm (gesturing, movements, placements etc.)
- Pausing
- Accents
- Fillers (um, ah, oh, etc.)

The Power of Reflection and Discussion: Best Teaching Practices for Pragmatics

To optimize learning, it is essential to account for reflection time to assess the usability of learned pragmatic skills. Reflections are essential in order to gain optimum comprehension of pragmatic concepts. Journaling will allow students to write down their thoughts as they go through the activities.

Students should be instructed to journal before, during or after each section. The length of the journal should be up to the student as each student will have their own unique connection with the lesson. Understanding of the concepts and questions can then be discussed in order to gain complete comprehension. This will assist in the principles being put into practice more frequently and carryover will occur in other environments.

Here is a list of reflection starters:

1. I am confident I will be able to use _____ when _____

2. If I knew _____ when _____, I could have _____

3. I now know _____

4. I use _____ when I am upset.

5. Pragmatics has helped me to _____

6. I would like to teach my _____ all about Pragmatics.

7. "It's not what you say" means _____

8. "It's how you say it" means _____

9. If I could do a commercial for "Pragmatics" I would say "_____".

10. The one thing I use all the time from the "Pragmatics Program is _____

11. I have learned a lot about _____

Discussions:
Pragmatic skills are predominately used for effective verbal/non-verbal communication. Therefore, it is not necessary to require lengthy writing assignments; the major benefit of this program is developed by active discussion, roll play, speaking and listening. Single word answers and short phrases are sufficient for all activities.

PRAGMATICS CULPRITS

- Facial Expressions
- Facial Grimaces
- Eye rolling
- Head nodding
- Body posturing (slumping, slouching, etc.)
- Turning your head and/or body away from the speaker
- Sucking in air
- Blowing out air loudly
- Pitch and Tone of voice
- Sing–song voice
- Inflections and volume of the voice
- Invasion of personal body space
- Hand and arm (gesturing, movements, placements etc.)
- Pausing
- Accents
- Fillers (um, ah, oh, etc.)

Which five culprits cause you the most frustration during communication with others?

For Me:	For Others:
1. _____	1. _____
2. _____	2. _____
3. _____	3. _____
4. _____	4. _____
5. _____	5. _____

NOTES

Listen for the difference in each sentence when you change pragmatic behaviors. How did you say it?

I have learned a lot being in your class.

I have learned a lot being in your class.

I have learned a lot being in your class.

I have learned a lot being in your class.

I have learned a lot being in your class.

I have learned a lot being in your class.

I have learned a lot being in your class.

I have learned a lot being in your class.

Thoughts:
_____
_____
_____
_____

NOTES

Listen for the difference in each sentence when you change pragmatic behaviors. How did you say it?

<u>I</u> apologize for my rude behavior.

I <u>apologize</u> for my rude behavior.

I apologize <u>for</u> my rude behavior.

I apologize for <u>my</u> rude behavior.

I apologize for my <u>rude</u> behavior.

I apologize for my rude <u>behavior.</u>

Thoughts:
_____
_____
_____

NOTES

Listen for the difference in each sentence when you change pragmatic behaviors. How did you say it?

<u>You</u> need to complete your work.

You <u>need</u> to complete your work.

You need <u>to</u> complete your work.

You need to <u>complete</u> your work.

You need to complete <u>your</u> work.

You need to complete your <u>work</u>.

Thoughts:
_____
_____
_____
_____

NOTES

Listen for the difference in each sentence when you change pragmatic behaviors. How did you say it?

<u>I</u> hope you will accept my apology.

I <u>hope</u> you will accept my apology.

I hope <u>you</u> will accept my apology.

I hope you <u>will</u> accept my apology.

I hope you will <u>accept</u> my apology.

I hope you will accept <u>my</u> apology.

I hope you will accept my <u>apology</u>.

Thoughts:
_____
_____
_____
_____

NOTES

Listen for the difference in each sentence when you change pragmatic behaviors. How did you say it?

<u>I</u> really enjoy working with you.

I <u>really</u> enjoy working with you.

I really <u>enjoy</u> working with you.

I really enjoy <u>working</u> with you.

I really enjoy working <u>with</u> you.

I really enjoy working with <u>you</u>.

Thoughts:
_____
_____
_____

NOTES

Listen for the difference in each sentence when you change pragmatic behaviors. How did you say it?

<u>Please</u> raise your hand before you speak.

Please <u>raise</u> your hand before you speak.

Please raise <u>your</u> hand before you speak.

Please raise your <u>hand</u> before you speak.

Please raise your hand <u>before</u> you speak.

Please raise your hand before <u>you</u> speak.

Please raise your hand before you <u>speak</u>.

Thoughts: _____
_____
_____

NOTES

Try creating a sentence of your own that can illustrate how emphasizing a word changes the meaning. How did you say it? Rewrite the sentence several times and underline words that can be emphasized.

NOTES

Notate what messages you get when each of these nonverbal ques are expressed to you.

Facial Expressions

Facial Grimaces

Eye Rolling

Lack of Eye Contact

Notate what messages you get when each of these nonverbal ques are expressed to you.

Turning head away from speaker	**Sucking in air loudly**
Inflections and volumes of the voice	**Pitch and tone of voice**

21

Notate what messages you get when each of these nonverbal ques are expressed to you.

Invasion of personal body space

Hand/arm (placement, gestures, movement)

Body posturing (Slumping, Slouching, etc.

Pausing

NOTES

PLEASANT FEELINGS

OPEN
Understanding
Confident
Reliable
Easy
Amazed
Free
Sympathetic
Interested
Satisfied

HAPPY
Great
Gay
Joyous
Lucky
Fortunate
Delighted
Overjoyed
Gleeful
Thankful
Important
Festive
Ecstatic
Satisfied
Glad
Cheerful
Sunny
Merry
Elated
Jubilant

ALIVE
Playful
Courageous
Energetic
Liberated
Optimistic
Provocative
Impulsive

GOOD
Calm
Peaceful
At ease
Comfortable
Pleased
Encouraged
Clever
Surprised
Content
Quiet
Certain
Relaxed
Serene
Free and easy
Bright
Blessed

PLEASANT FEELINGS

LOVE	**INTERESTED**	**POSITIVE**	**STRONG**
Loving	Concerned	Eager	Impulsive
Considerate	Affected	Keen	Free
Affectionate	Fascinated	Earnest	Sure
Sensitive	Intrigued	Intent	Certain
Tender	Absorbed	Anxious	Rebellious
Devoted	Inquisitive	Inspired	Unique
Attracted	Nosy	Determined	Dynamic
Passionate	Snoopy	Excited	Tenacious
Admiration	Engrossed	Enthusiastic	Hardy
Warm	Curious	Bold	Secure
Touched		Brave	
Sympathy		Daring	
Close		Challenged	
Loved		Optimistic	
Comforted		Re-enforced	
Drawn toward		Confident	
		Hopeful	

DIFFICULT/UNPLEASANT FEELINGS

INDIFFERENT	AFRAID	HURT	SAD
Insensitive	Fearful	Crushed	Tearful
Dull	Terrified	Tormented	Sorrowful
Nonchalant	Suspicious	Deprived	Pained
Neutral	Anxious	Pained	Grief
Reserved	Alarmed	Tortured	Anguish
Weary	Panic	Dejected	Desolate
Bored	Nervous	Rejected	Desperate
Preoccupied	Scared	Injured	Pessimistic
Cold	Worried	Offended	Unhappy
Disinterested	Frightened	Afflicted	Lonely
Lifeless	Timid	Aching	Grieved
	Shaky	Victimized	Mournful
	Restless	Heartbroken	Dismayed
	Doubtful	Agonized	
	Threatened	Appalled	
	Cowardly	Humiliated	
	Quaking	Wronged	
	Menaced	Alienated	
	Wary		

NOTES

Group Activities

1. Look through magazines to find pictures that demonstrate nonverbal clues.

2. Paste pictures on a posterboard to describe each nonverbal clues.

3. Discuss what you learned with the rest of your group. Each member of the group should take no more than 1 minute.

4. Design a group project that will give information on what you have learned.

5. Design a commercial to explain why you should use Pragmatics. (30 second maximum)

6. Watch a video or movie and point out the pragmatics culprits used.

7. In a group, have each student discuss which pragmatic action /culprits give the best results, and which one gives the worst results.

8. Have students brainstorm why it is important to learn and use pragmatics appropriately.

9. Have the students role play *before* and *after* skits showing the use of positive versus negative pragmatic behavior.

10. On a large poster/banner, give each student the opportunity to pledge by signing to utilize appropriate pragmatics.

NOTES

A Star Is Born

Directions: Cut out the Pragmatics Culprits below and place them in a container, bag, or box. Each participant will pull a culprit from the bag and act out or describe the culprit that they pulled.

Facial Expressions	Facial Grimaces	Eye Rolling
Fillers (um, a, o, etc.)	Lack of eye contact	Head Nodding
Sucking in air loudly	Sing-song voice	Pausing
Accents	Body posture (slumping, slouching, etc.)	Voice (tone, pitch, inflection)
Turning your head and/or body away from the speaker	Hand and arm (gesturing, movements, placements, etc.)	Invasion of personal body space

NOTES

S.S.S (THE THREE S'S)

S.S.S is a technique to assist in dealing with difficult situations. Before entering into a confrontation stop, step back and survey the situation. Create a comic book scenario that utilizes S.S.S in the correct order.

NOTES

Information can be presented in a negative, positive, or neutral manner dependent on how it is presented within the statement or conversation. Below is a list of all of the culprits. Place each culprit in the appropriate column. Remember some of them can be placed in more than one column.

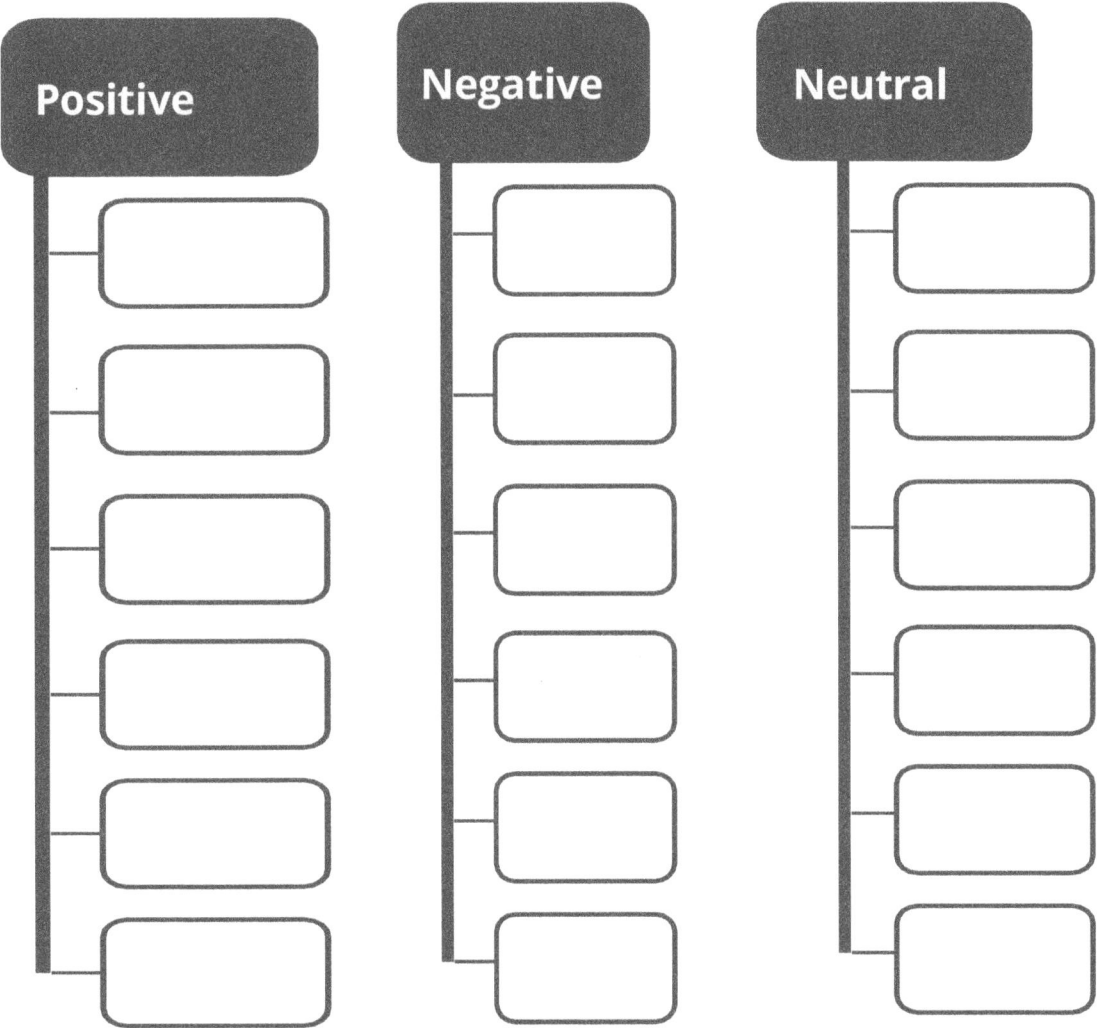

Facial Expressions	**Sucking in air**	**Invasion of personal body space**
Facial Grimaces	**Blowing out air loudly**	**Hand and arm**
Eye rolling	**Pitch and Tone of voice**	**Pausing**
Head Nodding	**Sing-song voice**	**Accents**
Body Posture	**Inflections and volume of voice**	**Fillers**
Turning your head and/or body away from the speaker		

NOTES

WHAT DO YOU HEAR? WHAT DO YOU SEE?

93% of communication is nonverbal. The communication culprits are communicated by what you see or what you hear. Underline the culprits that you hear. Place the culprits that you see in the boxes below.

Facial Expressions	**Sucking in air**	**Invasion of personal body space**
Facial Grimaces	**Blowing out air loudly**	**Hand and arm**
Eye rolling	**Pitch and Tone of voice**	**Pausing**
Head Nodding	**Sing-song voice**	**Accents**
Body Posture	**Inflections and volume of voice**	**Fillers**
Turning your head and/or body away from the speaker		

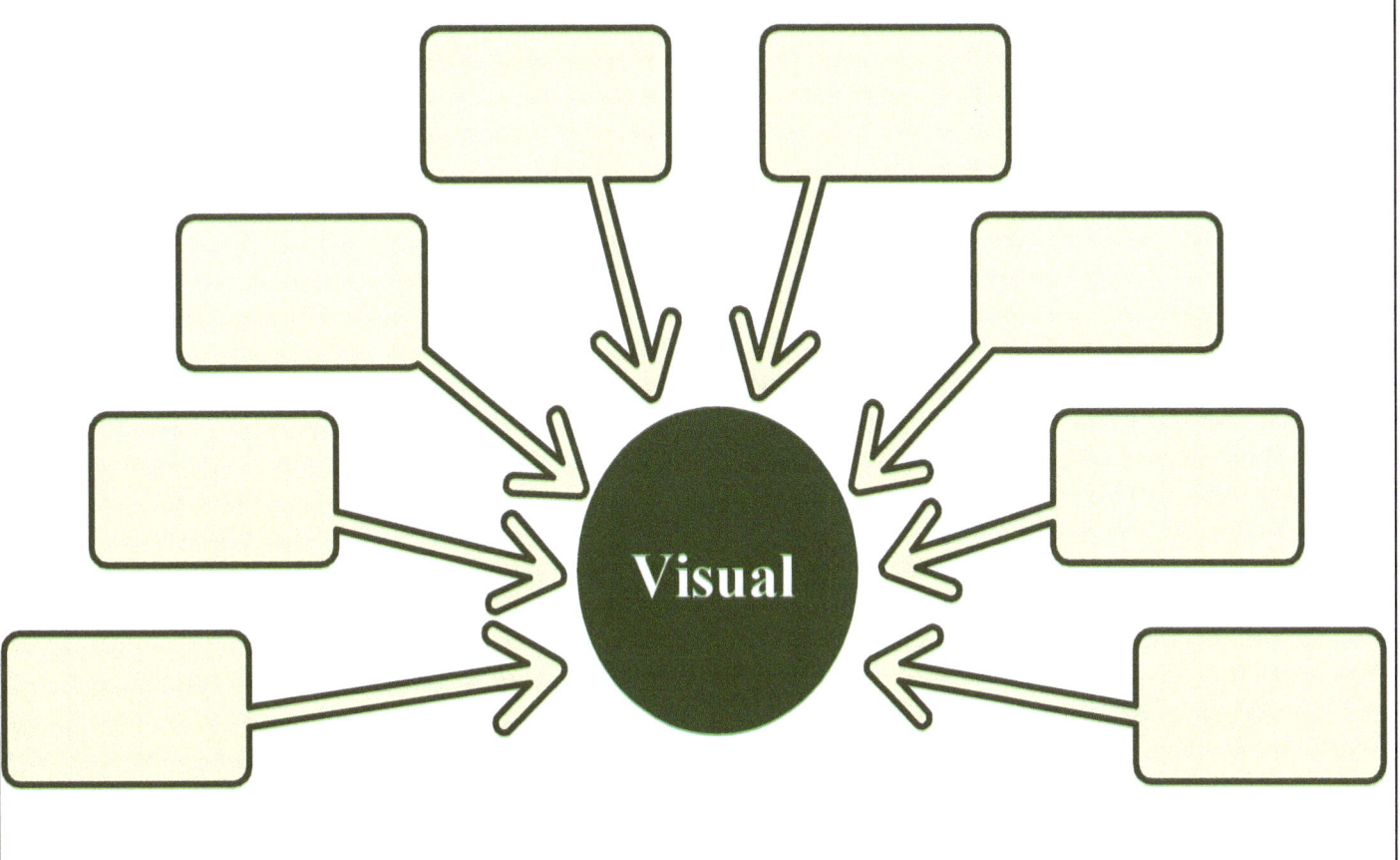

NOTES

Facial Expressions

Illustrate the culprit

Find a picture of the culprit.

How do you feel when expressing this culprit?   How do you feel when receiving this culprit?

Describe a situation where you observed or used this culprit?
_____
_____
_____
_____

Facial Grimaces

Illustrate the culprit

Find a picture of the culprit

How do you feel when expressing this culprit?   How do you feel when receiving this culprit?

Describe a situation where you observed or used this culprit?
_____
_____
_____
_____

Eye Rolling

Illustrate the culprit

Find a picture of the culprit

How do you feel when expressing this culprit?

How do you feel when receiving this culprit?

Describe a situation where you observed or used this culprit?
_____
_____
_____
_____

Head Nodding

Illustrate the culprit	Find a picture of the culprit

How do you feel when expressing this culprit?   How do you feel when receiving this culprit?

Describe a situation where you observed or used this culprit?
_____
_____
_____
_____

Body Posturing

Illustrate the culprit

Find a picture of the culprit

How do you feel when expressing this culprit?   How do you feel when receiving this culprit?

Describe a situation where you observed or used this culprit?
_____
_____
_____
_____

Turning Your Head/Body Away From the Speaker

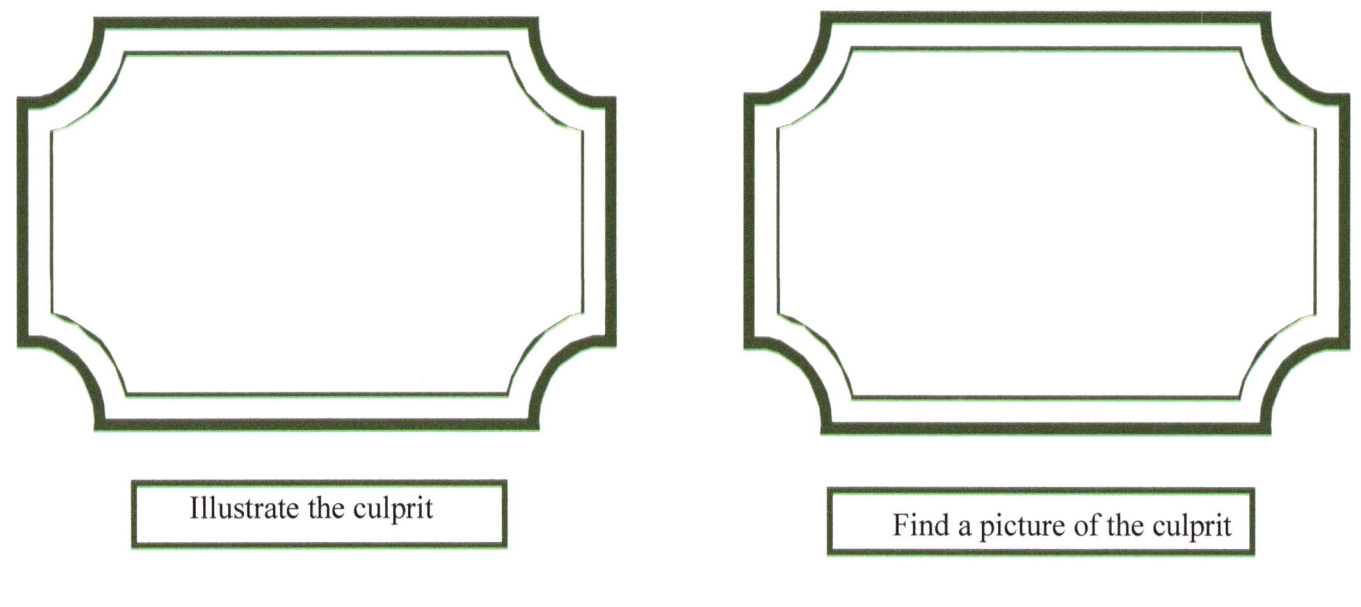

Illustrate the culprit

Find a picture of the culprit

How do you feel when expressing this culprit?

How do you feel when receiving this culprit?

Describe a situation where you observed or used this culprit?
_____
_____
_____
_____

Sucking In Air/ Blowing Out Air loudly

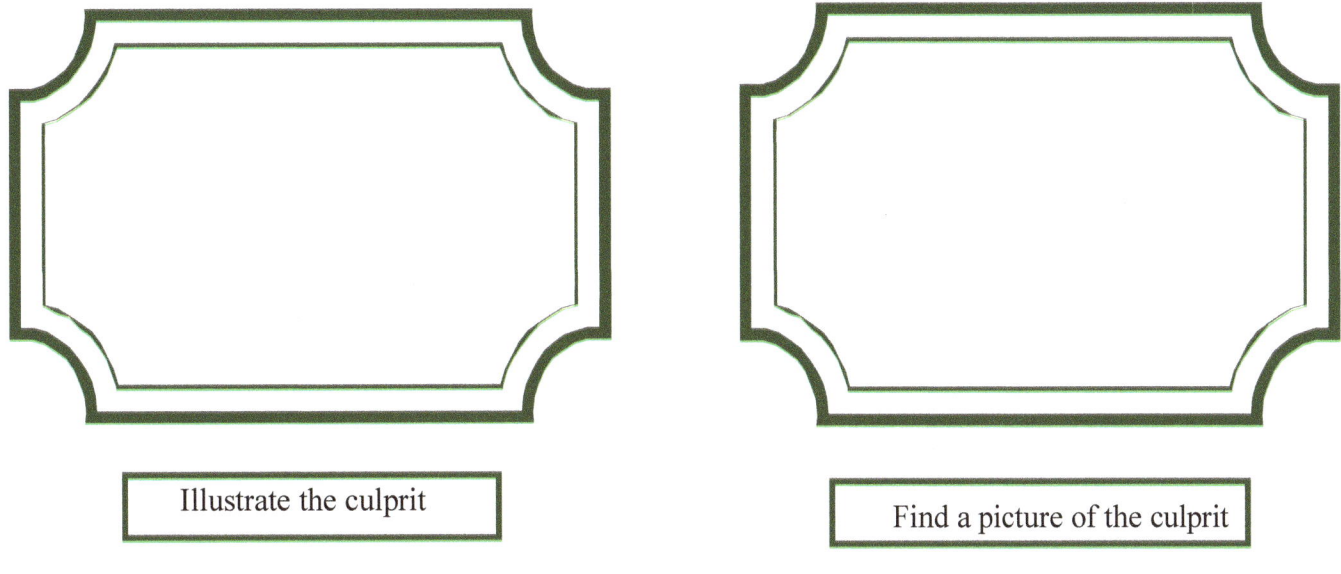

Illustrate the culprit

Find a picture of the culprit

How do you feel when expressing this culprit?

How do you feel when receiving this culprit?

Describe a situation where you observed or used this culprit?
_____
_____
_____
_____

Pitch and Tone of Voice

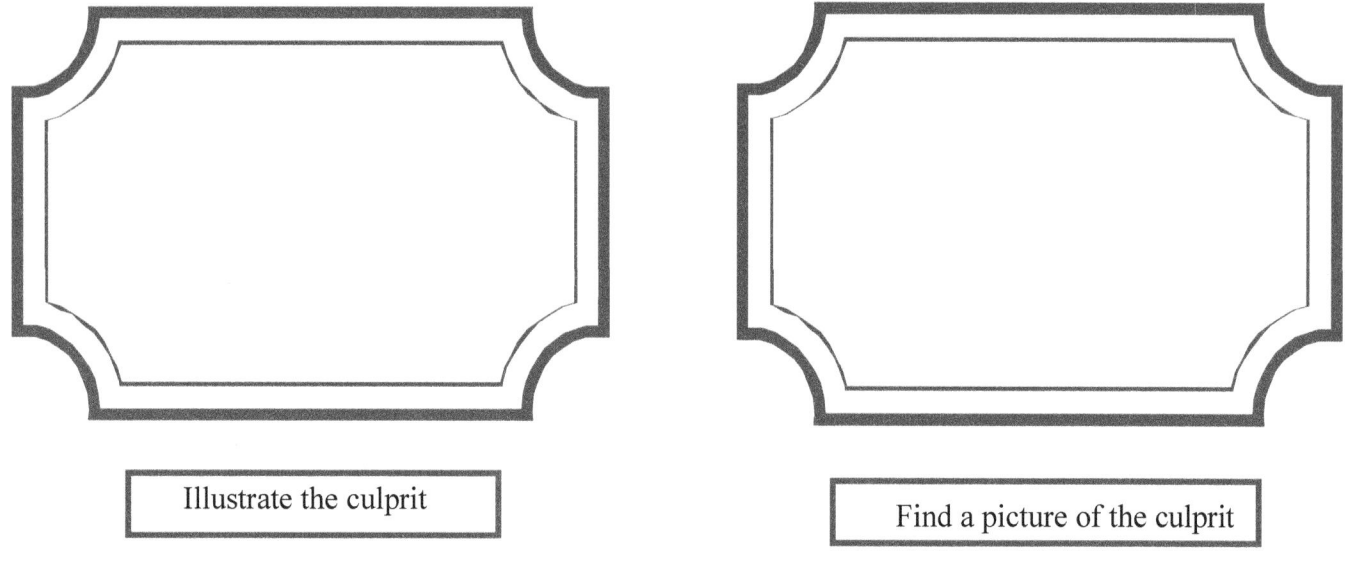

Illustrate the culprit

Find a picture of the culprit

How do you feel when expressing this culprit?   How do you feel when receiving this culprit?

Describe a situation where you observed or used this culprit?
_____
_____
_____
_____

Sing-Song Voice

Illustrate the culprit

Find a picture of the culprit

How do you feel when expressing this culprit?   How do you feel when receiving this culprit?

Describe a situation where you observed or used this culprit?
_____
_____
_____
_____

Inflections and Volume

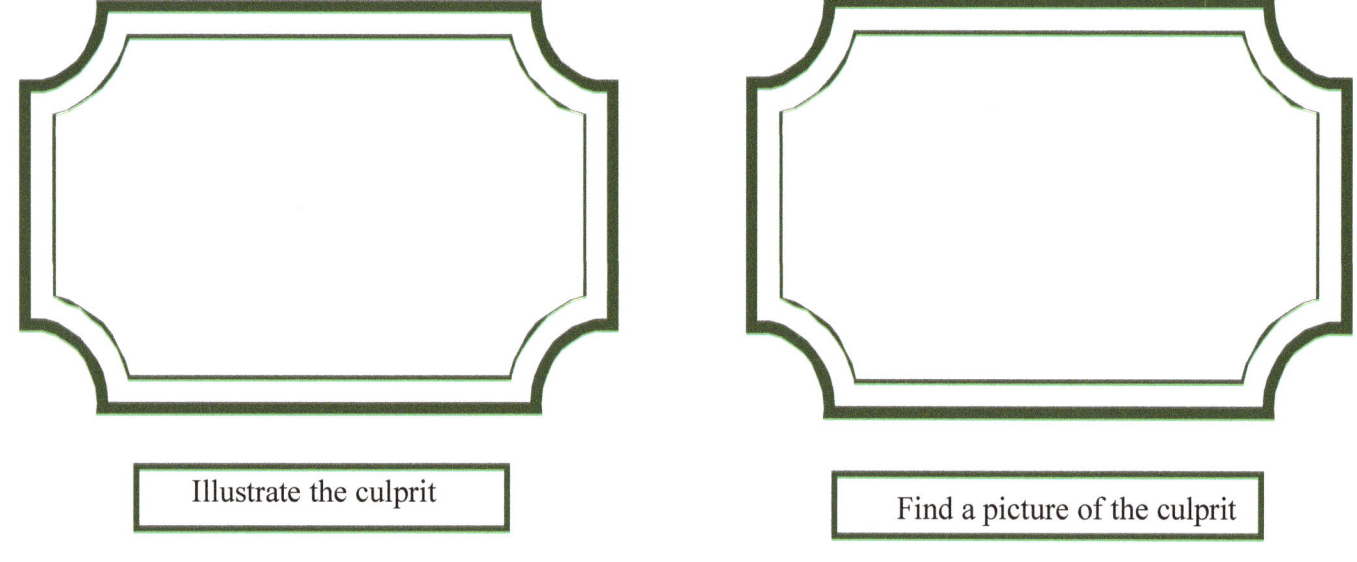

| Illustrate the culprit | Find a picture of the culprit |

How do you feel when expressing this culprit?   How do you feel when receiving this culprit?

Describe a situation where you observed or used this culprit?
_____
_____
_____
_____

Invasion of Personal Space

Illustrate the culprit

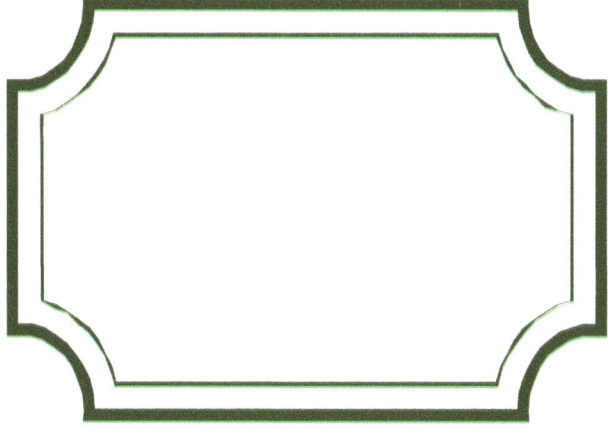

Find a picture of the culprit

How do you feel when expressing this culprit?

How do you feel when receiving this culprit?

Describe a situation where you observed or used this culprit?
_____
_____
_____
_____

Hand and Arm

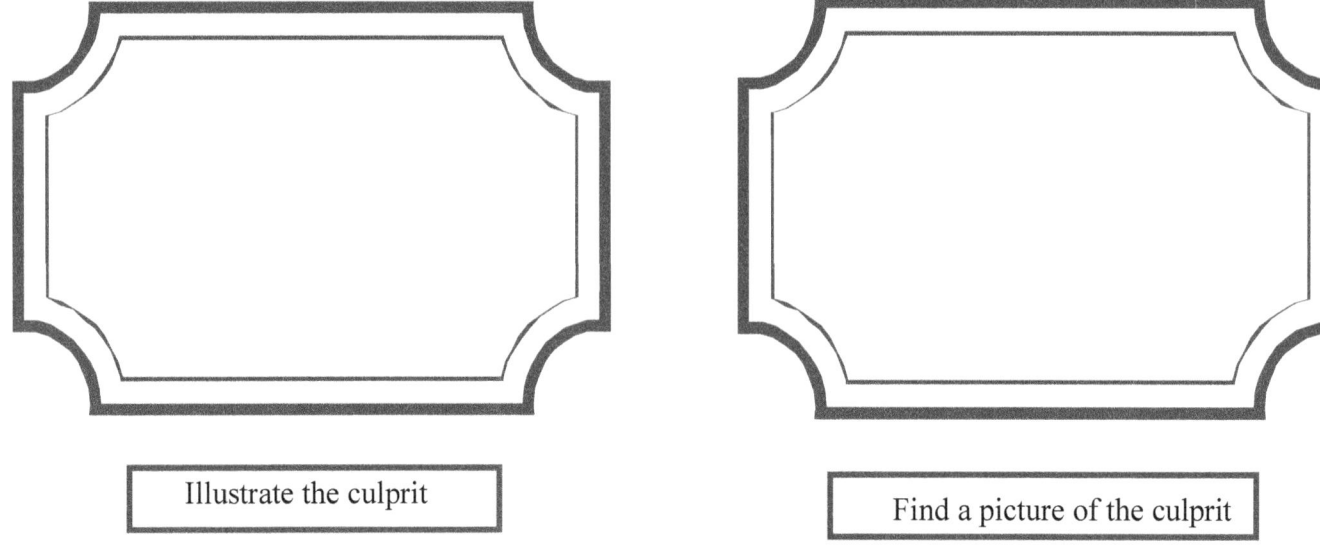

| Illustrate the culprit | Find a picture of the culprit |

How do you feel when expressing this culprit?   How do you feel when receiving this culprit?

Describe a situation where you observed or used this culprit?
_____
_____
_____
_____

Pausing

Illustrate the culprit

Find a picture of the culprit

How do you feel when expressing this culprit?   How do you feel when receiving this culprit?

Describe a situation where you observed or used this culprit?
_____
_____
_____
_____

Accents

Illustrate the culprit

Find a picture of the culprit

How do you feel when expressing this culprit?   How do you feel when receiving this culprit?

Describe a situation where you observed or used this culprit?
_____
_____
_____
_____

Fillers

Illustrate the culprit

Find a picture of the culprit

How do you feel when expressing this culprit?   How do you feel when receiving this culprit?

Describe a situation where you observed or used this culprit?
_____
_____
_____
_____

NOTES

NOTES

NOTES

NOTES

NOTES

About the Author

Natasha Boyd is an expert in the field of Speech Pathology. She has worked with students and clients from infancy to adulthood. Natasha holds a master's degree in Speech Pathology with a Minor in Audiology as well as a Lifetime Clinical Rehabilitative Services Credential. She has spent over three decades in the public school system. After recognizing the struggles that her middle school students faced in communicating their needs, Natasha developed a program to improve their non-verbal communication, known as "The Pragmatics Lady." Natasha has delivered her Pragmatics program to thousands of K-12 students and staff throughout California. Additionally, Natasha has trained college students and small business owners.

www.ingramcontent.com/pod-product-compliance
Lightning Source LLC
Chambersburg PA
CBHW061113070526
44583CB00027B/3281